KT-502-615

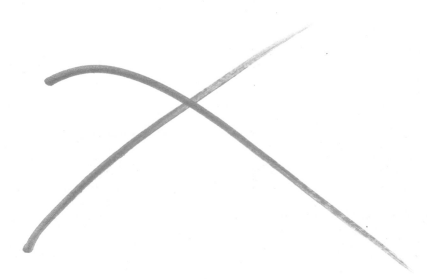

THE SEASONAL CAT

by the same author

THE ESSENTIAL CAT
With a Foreword by Doris Lessing

THE SEASONAL CAT

Thomas Wester

SOUVENIR PRESS

Copyright © 1989 by Thomas Wester

Originally published in Sweden by Trevi Publishers
as a calendar under the title *Katter året Runt*
First British edition published 1989 by Souvenir Press Ltd,
43 Great Russell Street, London WC1B 3PA
and simultaneously in Canada

All Rights Reserved. No part of this publication
may be reproduced, stored in a retrieval system,
or transmitted, in any form or by any means, electronic,
mechanical, photocopying, recording or otherwise without
the prior permission of the Copyright owner

ISBN 0 285 62954 9

Printed and bound in Great Britain by
WBC Print Ltd, Bristol and Maesteg

THE SPRING CAT

Stately, kindly, lordly friend
　　Condescend
Here to sit by me, and turn
Glorious eyes that smile and burn,
Golden eyes, love's lustrous meed,
On the golden page I read.

All your wondrous wealth of hair,
　　Dark and fair,
Silken-shaggy, soft and bright
As the clouds and beams of night,
Pays my reverent hand's caress
Back with friendlier gentleness.

From 'To a Cat'
ALGERNON CHARLES SWINBURNE
(1837–1909)

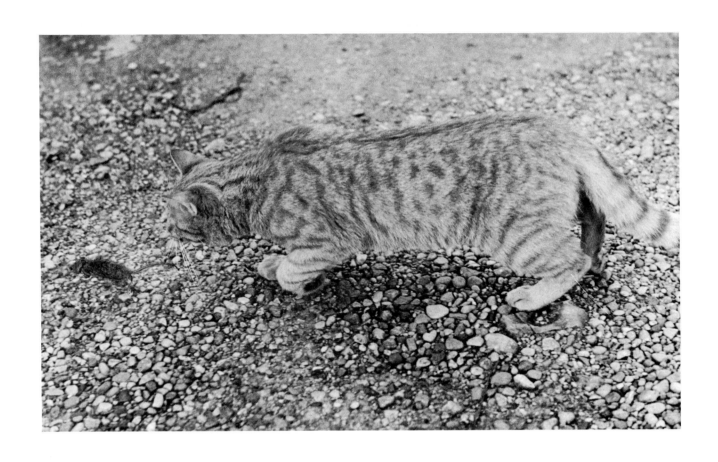

THE SUMMER CAT

Dear creature by the fire a-purr
   Strange idol, eminently bland,
Miraculous puss! As o'er your fur
   I trail a negligible hand . . .

An exquisite enchantment falls
   About the portals of my sense;
Meandering through enormous halls
   I breathe luxurious frankincense.

An ampler air, a warmer June
   Enfold me, and my wondering eye
Salutes a more imperial moon
   Throned in a more resplendent sky

Than ever knew this northern shore.
   Oh, strange! For you are with me too,
And I, who am a cat once more,
   Follow the woman that was you.

From 'The Cat'
GILES LYTTON STRACHEY
(1880–1932)

THE AUTUMN CAT

Cat! who hast pass'd thy grand climacteric,
   How many mice and rats hast in thy days
   Destroyed? How many titbits stolen? Gaze
With those bright languid segments green, and prick
Those velvet ears — but pr'ythee do not stick
   Thy latent talons in me — and upraise
   Thy gentle mew — and tell me all thy frays,
Of fish and mice, and rats and tender chick.
Nay, look not down, nor lick thy dainty wrists —
   For all thy wheezy asthma — and for all
Thy tail's tip is nick'd off — and though the fists
   Of many a maid have given thee many a maul,
Still is that fur as soft, as when the lists
   In youth thou enter'dest on glass bottled wall.

'To Mrs Reynolds' Cat'
JOHN KEATS
(1795–1821)

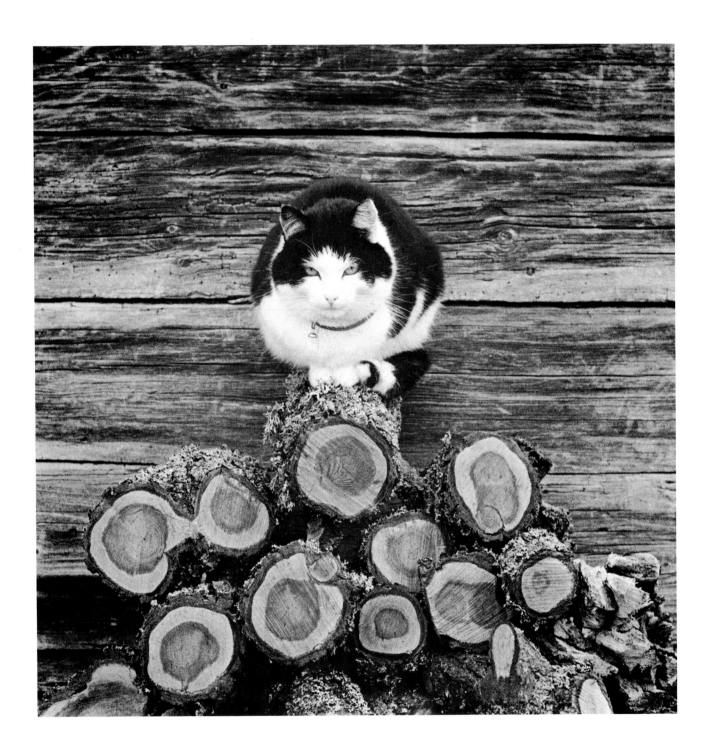

THE WINTER CAT

When the tea is brought at five o'clock,
and all the neat curtains are drawn with care,
The little black cat with bright green eyes
Is suddenly purring there.

At first she pretends, having nothing to do,
She has come in merely to blink by the grate,
But though tea may be late or the milk may be sour,
She is never late . . .

The white saucer like some full moon descends
At last from the cloud of the table above;
She sighs and dreams and thrills and glows,
Transfigured with love . . .

A long dim ecstasy holds her life;
Her world is an infinite shapeless white,
Till her tongue has curled the last holy drop
Then she sinks back into the night,

Draws and dips her body to heap
Her sleepy nerves in the great arm-chair,
Lies defeated and buried deep
Three or four hours unconscious there.

From 'Milk for the Cat'
HAROLD MONRO
(1879-1932)

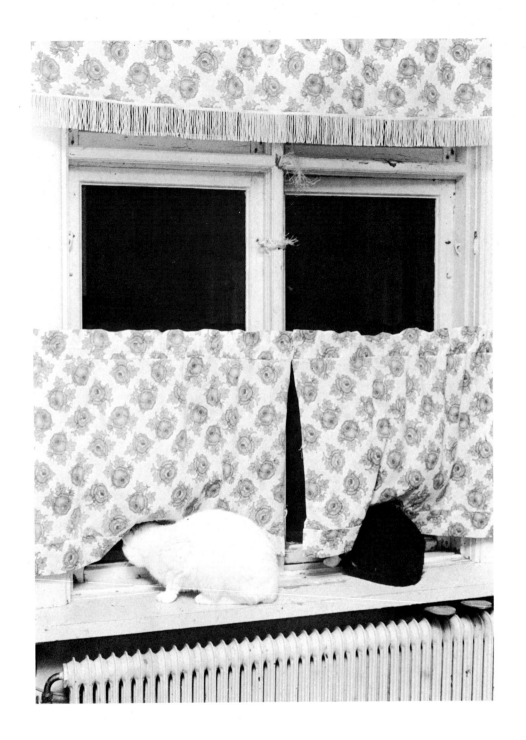